THE WISDOM OF SCIENCE
SCIENCE IN SOUND BITES

Robert W. Fuller

ISBN: 1502354276
ISBN-13: 978-1502354273

Cover Credit: The base image is a faithful photographic reproduction of a two-dimensional, public domain work of art. Camille Flammarion, L'Atmosphere: Météorologie Populaire (Paris, 1888). The image has been re-colored for the specific use of the cover of this book.

Robert W. Fuller's web site: www.robertworksfuller.com
Dignity Movement: www.breakingranks.net
Huffington Post: www.huffingtonpost.com/robert-fuller

For readers who want to explore dignity as a foundation for interpersonal and international relations, Robert W. Fuller's novel The Rowan Tree *is now available as an ebook, a paperback, and an audiobook at: www.rowantreenovel.com*

To my father

Calvin S. Fuller

who showed how science could illuminate
not just the world around us,
but also the world within.

.

*Live your life as if there are no miracles
and everything is a miracle.*

– Albert Einstein

Table of Contents

INTRODUCTION

In the few centuries since our understanding of Nature turned scientific, both our lives and our lifespans have changed more than in the previous hundred-thousand years.

Leave aside the issue of whether science has made our lives better or worse. What's not in dispute is that the percentage of people who reject its fruits—electricity, antibiotics, cars, planes, phones, and all the rest—is vanishingly small.

I've had a lifelong interest in understanding why *objective* scientific inquiry works and how it relates to our subjective sense of "What's right?" and "What's beautiful?" To those ends, I've collected aphorisms, maxims, and *mots justes* that shed light on the nature of science. My goal is not to press a particular view of science, but rather to reflect the range of scientists' personalities and the various truth-seeking strategies they employ.

This collection of aphorisms is offered in the spirit of Ralph Waldo Emerson's observation that "it is not instruction, but provocation, that I can receive from another." If these sayings provoke you to ask "What is science? What is it not? Why does it work?" and "How does science relate to morality and religion?" then it will have served its purpose.

In the name of readability, I've taken the liberty of omitting extraneous or redundant language from a few of the quotes, but in no case has the meaning been altered.

1. WHAT IS SCIENCE?

Aristotle could have avoided the mistake of thinking that women have fewer teeth than men by the simple device of asking Mrs. Aristotle to open her mouth.

— Bertrand Russell (1872–1970), Welsh mathematician and philosopher

Know you what it is to be a child? ... it is to believe in belief.

— Francis Thompson, 19th c. British poet

There are in fact two things—science and opinion; the former begets knowledge, the latter ignorance.

– Hippocrates (c. 460–377 BCE), Greek physician, father of medicine, author of the Hippocratic Oath: "Do No Harm"

I appeal to your own eyes as my witness and judge.

– William Harvey (1578–1657), English physician and discoverer of the circulation of the blood. His simple appeal—that people look for themselves, rather than to authority—was revolutionary in his time. His discovery furthered not only physiology, but also the scientific method in general. The idea that theological dogma be subordinated to the empirical experience of the individual was a crucial step in the birth of science—and of democracy.

It is a test of true theories not only to account for, but to predict, phenomena.

– William Whewell (1794–1866), English scholar who taught the scientific method at a time when it was a novelty, and put his finger on a key element—*prediction*.

Science is built up with facts, as a house is with stones. But a collection of facts is no more a science than a heap of stones is a house.

The advance of science is not comparable to the changes of a city, where old edifices are pitilessly torn down to give place to new, but to the continuous evolution of zoological types which develop ceaselessly and end by becoming unrecognizable to the common sight, but where an expert eye finds always traces of the prior work of the past centuries.

— Jules Henri Poincaré (1854–1912), French mathematician and philosopher of science

Common sense is, as a matter of fact, nothing more than layers of preconceived notions stored in our memories and emotions for the most part before age eighteen.

The whole of science is nothing more than a refinement of everyday thinking.

Science is the attempt to make the chaotic diversity of our sense-experience correspond to a logically uniform system of thought.

— Albert Einstein (1879–1955), German-born American physicist, in a class by himself

The stumbling way in which even the ablest scientists in every generation have had to fight through thickets of erroneous observations, misleading generalizations, inadequate formulations, and unconscious prejudice is rarely appreciated by those who obtain their scientific knowledge from textbooks.

— James B. Conant (1893–1978), American chemist, educator, and scientific statesman

Science is a cemetery of dead ideas, even though life may issue from them.

True science teaches, above all, to doubt and be ignorant.

— Miguel de Unamuno (1864–1936), Spanish philosopher

That is the essence of science: ask an impertinent question, and you are on the way to a pertinent answer.

– Jacob Bronowski (1908–1974), Polish-born British Renaissance Man, creator of the television series, *The Ascent of Man*

Science commits suicide when it adopts a creed.

– Thomas Henry Huxley (1825–1895), English biologist and early champion of Darwin's theory of evolution

Science is a collection of successful recipes.

– Paul Valéry (1871–1945), French critic. This characterization may seem simplistic, but it has two virtues: it emphasizes the operational character of scientific theories and it provides a nice antidote to the besetting sins of modern science: arrogance and grandiosity.

The basic texture of research consists of dreams into which the threads of reasoning, measurement, and calculation are woven.

– Albert Szent-Györgyi (1893–1986), Hungarian-born American biochemist who isolated vitamin C.

O speculators about perpetual motion, how many vain chimeras have you created in the like quest? Go and take your place with the seekers after gold.

— Leonardo da Vinci (1452–1519), Italian artist and engineer. Here he anticipates the law of conservation of energy: "There is no free lunch in Nature."

This is the excellent foppery of the world, that, when we are sick in fortune—often the surfeits of our own behavior—we make guilty of our disasters the sun, the moon, and stars; as if we were villains by necessity, fools by heavenly compulsion, knaves, thievers, and treachers by spherical predominance, drunkards, liars, and adulterers by an enforced obedience of planetary influence.

— William Shakespeare (1564–1616). In these lines from *King Lear* Shakespeare mocks astrological beliefs, as he does in the better known line from *Julius Caesar*, "The fault, dear Brutus, is not in our stars, but in ourselves..."

We are to admit no more causes of natural things than such as are both true and sufficient to explain their appearances.

Nature does nothing in vain, and more is in vain when less will serve; for Nature is pleased with simplicity, and affects not the pomp of superfluous causes.

I do not make hypotheses.

– Isaac Newton (1642–1727), English scientist and mathematician, discoverer of laws of motion and gravitation and the calculus. Newton is insisting that one need not deal in speculation. He held that metaphysical "hypotheses" were unnecessary and extraneous and had no place in scientific theorizing. His method became the model for physics: Discover Nature's laws, express them mathematically, and derive consequences and predictions.

The sciences do not try to explain, they hardly even try to interpret, they mainly make models. By a model is meant a mathematical construct which, with the addition of certain verbal interpretations, describes observed phenomena. The justification of such a mathematical construct is solely and precisely that it is expected to work.

– John von Neumann (1903–1957), Hungarian-born American mathematician, creator of game theory, and logician of digital computers

Man is a creature who makes pictures of himself, and then comes to resemble the picture.

– Iris Murdoch (1919–1999), British author and philosopher

*It is not a question of whether a theory is philosophically delightful, or easy to understand, or perfectly reasonable from the point of view of common sense. The theory of quantum electrodynamics describes Nature as **absurd** from the point of view of common sense. And it agrees fully with experiment. So I hope you can accept Nature as She is — absurd. ... Please don't turn yourself off because you can't believe Nature is so strange.*

– Richard P. Feynman (1918–1988), Nobel-laureate American physicist, who demonstrated on national television that frozen O-rings had led to the explosion of the Challenger space shuttle.

Under normal conditions the research scientist is not an innovator but a solver of puzzles, and the puzzles upon which he concentrates are just those which he believes can be both stated and solved within the existing scientific tradition.

The transfer of allegiance from paradigm to paradigm is a conversion experience that cannot be forced. Though a generation is sometimes required to effect the change, scientific communities have again and again been converted to new paradigms. Furthermore, these conversions occur not despite the fact that scientists are human but because they are.

— Thomas Kuhn (1922–1996), American philosopher and historian of science who introduced the notion of "paradigm shift" to describe scientific revolutions

2. THE CREATIVE PROCESS

The most important of my discoveries have been suggested to me by my failures.

– Sir Humphrey Davy (1778–1829), English chemist who discovered the anesthetic effect of laughing gas, isolated metallic elements, and showed industrialists that investing in Research and Development ("R & D") paid off. Davy is one of the fathers of the age of technology.

It is the customary fate of new truths to begin as heresies and to end as superstitions.

– Thomas Henry Huxley (1825–1895), English biologist

The investigator should have a robust faith — and yet not believe.

The true worth of a researcher lies in pursuing what he did not seek in his experiment as well as what he sought.

    – Claude Bernard (1813–1878), French physiologist

We haven't got the money, so we've got to think!

    – Ernest Rutherford (1871–1937), British pioneer nuclear physicist

Firstly, gradualness. About this most important condition of fruitful scientific work I can never speak without emotion. Gradualness, gradualness, gradualness.

    – Ivan P. Pavlov (1849–1936), Russian physiologist who discovered the conditioned reflex experimenting with dogs

[As a student] I learned to scent out that which was able to lead to fundamentals and to

turn aside from the multitude of things which clutter up the mind and divert it from the essential. The hitch in this was, of course, that one had to cram all this stuff into one's mind for the examinations, whether one liked it or not. This coercion had such a deterring effect [upon me] that, after I had passed the final examination, I found the consideration of any scientific problems distasteful to me for an entire year. Such coercion smothers every truly scientific impulse. It is nothing short of a miracle that the modern methods of instruction have not yet entirely strangled the holy curiosity of inquiry; for this delicate little plant, aside from stimulation, stands mainly in need of freedom; without this it goes to wreck and ruin without fail. It is a very grave mistake to think that the enjoyment of seeing and searching can be promoted by means of coercion and a sense of duty. To the contrary, I believe that it would be possible to rob even a healthy beast of prey of its voraciousness, if it were possible, with the aid of a whip, to force the beast to devour continuously, even when not hungry.

Love is a better teacher than duty.

My pencil knows more than I do.
  – Albert Einstein (1879–1955). Bravo!

In any field, whether it's psychology or physics, find the strangest thing and then explore it.
  – John Archibald Wheeler (1911–1908), American physicist, pioneer in nuclear and gravitation physics

It is the lone worker who makes the first advance in a subject. The details may be worked out by a team, but the prime idea is due to the enterprise, thought, and perception of an individual.
  – Alexander Fleming (1881–1955), Scottish bacteriologist who discovered penicillin in 1928 (by instinctively following John Wheeler's advice)

I have to think very hard about a problem but this thinking never leads me anywhere; it is but a necessary priming process. Find-

ing myself unable to solve the problem, I let it sink into my subconscious. How long it stays there varies. Then, unexpectedly, the solution is passed into my conscious mind. My brain must have done as the Hungarian laxative which was advertised: "While you sleep it does the work."

– Albert Szent-Györgyi (1893–1986). His description of his creative process is remarkably like that given by French mathematician Jacques Hadamard (1865–1963) in his classic *The Psychology of Invention in the Mathematical Field.*

Basic research is when I'm doing what I don't know what I'm doing.

– Wernher von Braun (1912–1977), German and American rocket pioneer. Designed the V-2 and Saturn rockets.

The progress of science is strewn, like an ancient desert trail, with the bleached skeletons of discarded theories which once seemed to possess eternal life.

– Arthur Koestler (1905–1983), British author

It takes two to invent anything. The one makes up combinations; the other recognizes what is important in the mass of things which the former has imparted. What we call genius is much less the work of the first than the readiness of the second to grasp the value of what has been laid before him and to choose it.

– Paul Valéry (1871–1945), French critic

Depart, 'original' enthusiast!
How would this insight peeve you: whatsoever
A human being thinks, if dumb or clever,
Was thought before him in the past.

– Johann Wolfgang von Goethe (1749–1832), German Renaissance Man, sometimes described as "the last guy to know everything." The couplet shows that *he*, at least, knew his limits.

Science throws her treasures, not like a capricious fairy into the lap of a favored few, but into the laps of all humanity, with a lavish extravagance that no legend every dreamed of.

– Ernst Mach (1838–1916), Austrian physicist and philosopher

When you open a door, you look through and there are a hundred more doors. Step through the next one and there are a hundred more. The more we understand the more we comprehend the vastness of our ignorance.

– Sylvia Earle (1935–), American marine biologist who set a record for deepest solo untethered dive in the Pacific Ocean

An ass had the task of carrying the statue of Isis, and when the populace honored the statue by falling down before it, he thought the honor had been paid to him.

– Georg C. Lichtenberg (1742–1799), physicist and satirist. (Isis is the Egyptian Goddess of fertility. Lichtenberg's warning might well be engraved on science medals, like a Surgeon General's warning, against *the* occupational hazard of science—hubris.)

I can forgive Alfred Nobel for having invented dynamite, but only a fiend in human form could have invented the Nobel Prize.

– George Bernard Shaw (1856–1950), Irish dramatist

The Nobel prize will someday be a museum piece — like the crown.

– Peter Putnam (1926–1987), American physicist and philosopher

I found that the more I worked with chromosomes, the bigger and bigger they got, and when I was really working with them I wasn't outside. I was part of the system. I was right down there with them, and everything got big. I even was able to see the internal parts of chromosomes. It surprised me because I actually felt as if they were my friends ... As you look at these things, they become part of you. And you forget yourself.

People love to talk about themselves and their work, and I had an opportunity to listen. And I listened very carefully. I was being educated, and it was a great opportunity for me not to be listened to, but to listen.

– Barbara McClintock (1902-1992), American Nobel-laureate geneticist. She was on unusually intimate terms with the tiny objects she examined through her microscope and this in-

THE WISDOM OF SCIENCE

timacy was a source of her extraordinary observational power. She saw things no one had ever seen before and though it took thirty years for her revolutionary work on genetic transposition to be recognized, she eventually taught others to see them too.

It's an experience like no other experience, the best thing that can happen to a scientist, realizing that something that's happened in his or her mind exactly corresponds to something that happens in nature. It's startling every time it occurs. One is surprised that a construct of one's own mind can actually be realized in the honest-to-goodness world out there. A great shock and a great, great joy.

– Leo P. Kadanoff, contemporary American mathematical physicist, developer of chaos theory and fractals

I can say with certainty that the ablest students whom I met as a teacher were deeply interested in the theory of knowledge. I mean by "ablest students" those who excelled not only in skill but in independence

Robert W. Fuller

of judgment. They liked to start discussions about the axioms and methods of science and proved by their obstinacy in the defense of their opinions that this issue was important to them.

New theories are first of all necessary when we encounter new facts which cannot be "explained" by existing theories. But this motivation for setting up new theories is, so to speak, trivial, imposed from without. There is another, more subtle motive of no less importance. This is the striving toward unification and simplification of the premises of the theory as a whole.

— Albert Einstein (1879–1955)

Back of any discovery or invention there is invariably to be found an evolutionary development of ideas making its geniture possible. The history of the calculus furnishes a remarkably apt illustration. The method of Newton was no more unanticipated than were his laws of motion and gravitation.

[Newton and Leibniz] are to be thought of as the inventors of the calculus in the sense that they gave to the infinitesimal procedures of their predecessors the unity and precision necessary for further development. Their work differed from the methods of their predecessors, Barrow and Fermat, more in attitude and generality than in substance and detail. The procedures of Barrow and Fermat were themselves but elaborations of the views of such men as Torricelli, Cavalieri, and Galileo, or Kepler.

– Carl Boyer (1906–1976), historian of science and mathematics

Genius ... is not a biological fact. It is a combination of social conditions wherein the life story of the individual within the group and within his own family plays the determining role.

– Jean Rostand (1894–1977), French biologist and philosopher

3. SUCCESS AND FAILURE

Eureka!

– Archimedes (c. 287–212 BCE), Greek mathematician, upon discovering the principle of buoyancy, which bears his name.

Results? Why man, I have gotten a lot of results. I know 50,000 things that won't work.

– Thomas A. Edison (1847–1931), prolific American inventor who characterized genius as "one percent inspiration and ninety-nine percent perspiration."

Experience does not ever err, it is only your judgment that errs in promising itself results which are not caused by your experiments.

– Leonardo da Vinci (1452–1519), Italian artist and engineer, archetype of the "renaissance man"

I am enlightened, in the midst of a most desirable contemplation, eighteen months ago by the first glimmerings of dawn, three months ago by clear daylight, and just a few days ago by the sun itself. ...The die is cast; I will write my book and little does it matter whether it is read now or has to await posterity. I may well wait a hundred years for a reader, since God himself has waited six thousand years for someone to behold His work.

– Johann Kepler (1571–1630), German astronomer. While celebrating his discovery of the laws of planetary motion, which contradict Church doctrine, Kepler still accepts unquestioningly the Earth's Biblical age.

An expert is someone who knows some of the worst mistakes that can be made in a subject and how to avoid them.

– attributed both to German physicist Werner Heisenberg (1901–76), one of the creators of quantum theory, and to Danish physicist Niels Bohr (1885–1962), a pioneer in atomic physics

There are two sorts of truths: trivialities, whose opposites are obviously absurd, and profound truths, whose opposites are also profound truths.

– Niels Bohr. There are numerous reports of him appealing to this notion in conversations.

I think and think for months and years. Ninety-nine times, the conclusion is false. The hundredth time I am right.

No amount of experimentation can ever prove me right; a single experiment can prove me wrong.

– Albert Einstein (1879–1955). As of 2014, "Big Al," as he was reverently called by graduate students at Princeton, is still batting 1000.

Mistakes are often the stepping stones to utter failure.

— The WELL ("Whole Earth 'Lectronic Link," a public computer bulletin board). Mistakes may be survivable, even necessary, but they are hardly sufficient.

Research is the process of going up alleys to see if they are blind.

— Marston Bates (1906–1974), American zoologist

It's not enough for you to succeed; your colleagues must fail.

— Henry Foley (1917–1982), American physicist, quoting Gore Vidal, La Rochefoucauld, and, legend has it, Genghis Khan

I made my mistakes faster than others.

— Niels Bohr, offered as an explanation for his success to his collaborator John A. Wheeler. Together, they pioneered the liquid-drop model of nuclear fission.

Although I am fully convinced of the truth of the views given in this volume, I by no means expect to convince experienced naturalists whose minds are stocked with a multitude of facts all viewed, during a long course of years, from a point of view directly opposite to mine. But I look with confidence to the future—to young and rising naturalists, who will be able to view both sides of the question with impartiality.

  – Charles Darwin (1809–1882), English naturalist, originator of the theory of evolution by natural selection

I know that most men, including those at ease with problems of the greatest complexity, can seldom accept even the simplest and most obvious truth if it be such as would oblige them to admit the falsity of conclusions which they have delighted in explaining to colleagues, which they have proudly taught to others, and which they have woven, thread by thread, into the fabric of their lives.

  – Leo Tolstoy (1828–1910), Russian writer

I have had a conception today as revolutionary and as great as the kind of thought that Newton had.

A new scientific truth does not triumph by convincing its opponents and making them see the light, but rather because its opponents eventually die, and a new generation grows up that is familiar with it.

— Max Planck (1858–1947), German physicist, father of modern quantum theory. The growth of scientific consensus is more like the growth of political consensus than is sometimes realized.

We have discovered the secret of life!

— Francis Crick (1916–2004), English Nobel-laureate molecular biologist, co-discoverer (with James Watson) of the double helix structure of the gene

You must not attempt this approach to parallels. I have traversed this bottomless night, which extinguished all light and joy of my life. I entreat you, leave the science of paral-

lels alone. The ruin of my disposition and my fall date back to this time.

– Wolfgang Bolyai (1775–1856), Hungarian mathematician, advising his son János, who, fortunately, ignored this parental advice.

*It is now my plan to publish a work on parallels. I have discovered such wonderful things that I was amazed. When you, my dear Father, see them, you will understand...**that out of nothing I have created a strange new universe.***

– János Bolyai (1802–1860), replying to his father Wolfgang in 1823.

I have more things on my mind than most males with whom I must compete. I say 'must' because, as we all know, that is the way the research and management games are played. I do research and management for fun, but nevertheless I compete vigorously. And here again a woman is in trouble. She's damned if she does and damned if she doesn't. If she does not compete, it proves women can't do physics; if she does compete, she isn't feminine and hence, presumably, is some sort of freak.

— Betsy Ancker-Johnson (1927–   ), American physicist and a vice-president of General Motors

4. OUR PLACE IN THE UNIVERSE

The eternal silence of these infinite spaces frightens me.

– Blaise Pascal (1623–1662), French mathematician, physicist and philosopher

Anyone living in a house, if he is ignorant of its materials or construction, its size and kind, its position and distinguishing characteristics, is not worthy of being a guest in such a place. Similarly, he who is born and brought up in the hall of the universe, if he neglects to get to know the reason for its

Robert W. Fuller

wonderful beauty when he reaches maturity, is unworthy of that hall and, if it should be possible, must be thrust out of it.

— Adelard of Bath, 12th century English philosopher who introduced Arabic science to Europe

In the middle of all sits the Sun enthroned. In this most beautiful temple, could we place this luminary in any better position from which he can illuminate the whole at once? He is rightly called the Lamp, the Mind, the Ruler of the Universe. So the Sun sits as upon a royal throne, ruling his children, the planets which circle round him.

— Nicholas Copernicus (1473–1543), Polish astronomer whose model of the planets orbiting the sun challenged the prevailing earth-centered model. In its time this view was revolutionary and blasphemous. Copernicus's new cosmology—that the planets *revolve*—transformed both our sense of our place in the Universe and our sense of ourselves, and gave us the term "revolution" to describe such upheavals, whether scientific or political.

To consider the earth as the only populated world in infinite space is as absurd as to assert that in an entire field of millet, only one grain will grow.

– Metrodorus, Greek philosopher of the 4th century BCE

Our sun is one of 100 billion stars in our galaxy. Our galaxy is one of billions of galaxies populating the universe. It would be the height of presumption to think that we are the only living things in that enormous immensity.

– Wernher von Braun (1912–1977), German, and later, American rocket pioneer

The Earth is just too small and fragile a basket for the human race to keep all its eggs in.

– Robert Heinlein (1907–1988), American science fiction writer

Sooner or later every one of us breathes an atom that has been breathed before by anyone

*you can think of who has lived before us —
Michelangelo or George Washington or Moses.*

– Jacob Bronowski (1908–1974), Creator of
the television series *The Ascent of Man*

*From a human point of view, the difference
between the mind of a human being and that
of a mountain goat is wonderful; from the
point of view of the infinite ignorance that
surrounds us, the difference is not impressive.*

– Wendell Berry (1934–), American writer,
environmental activist, and farmer

*We had succeeded in showing that every-
thing is made of stardust. We were stardust.*

– Hans Bethe (1906–2005), German-born
American Nobel-laureate physicist who explained how nuclear reactions generate energy
in stars

The World would be a safer place,
If someone had a plan,
Before exploring Outer Space,
To find the Inner Man.

– Edgar Y. Harburg (1898–1981), American who wrote the words to the song "Over the Rainbow" for the film *The Wizard of Oz*

Viewed from the distance of the moon, the astonishing thing about the earth is that it is alive. Aloft, floating free beneath the moist, gleaming, membrane of bright blue sky, is the rising earth, the only exuberant thing in this part of the cosmos.

The uniformity of earth's life, more astonishing than its diversity, is accountable by the high probability that we derived, originally, from some single cell, fertilized in a bolt of lightning as the earth cooled.

It is from the progeny of this parent cell that we all take our looks; we still share genes around, and the resemblance of the enzymes of grasses to those of whales is in fact a family resemblance.

— Lewis Thomas (1913–1993), American biologist and writer

If you wish to make an apple pie from scratch, you must first invent the Universe.

— Carl Sagan (1934–1996), American astronomer, writer and creator of the television series *Cosmos*

All we know is still infinitely less than all that still remains unknown.

— William Harvey (1578–1657), English physician and discoverer of the circulation of the blood

The known is finite, the unknown infinite; intellectually we stand on an islet in the midst of an illimitable ocean of inexplicability. Our business in every generation is to reclaim a little more land, to add something to the extent and solidity of our possessions.

— Thomas Henry Huxley (1825–1895), English naturalist

The more the universe seems incomprehensible, the more it also seems pointless. The effort to understand the universe is one of the very few things that lifts human life a little above the level of farce and gives it some of the grace of tragedy.

   – Steven Weinberg (1933–   ), American Nobel-laureate physicist

[The] tyranny of the genes has lasted for three billion years and has been precariously overthrown only in the last hundred thousand years by a single species, **Homo sapiens**. *We have overthrown the tyranny by inventing symbolic language and culture. Our behavior patterns are now to a great extent culturally rather than genetically determined. We can choose to keep a defective gene in circulation because our culture tells us not to let hemophiliac children die. We have stolen back from our genes the freedom to make choices and to make mistakes.*

   – Freeman Dyson (1923–   ), British-born American physicist and writer

The universe is infinite in all directions, not only above us in the large but also below us in the small. If we start from our human scale of existence and explore the content of the universe further and further, we finally arrive, both in the large and in the small, at misty distances where first our senses and then even our concepts fail us.

— Emil Wiechert (1861–1928), German physicist, writing in 1896, as quoted by Freeman Dyson in his book *Infinite In All Directions*.

I just couldn't look at the sky without wondering how anyone could do anything but study the stars. Probably the greatest bliss I have ever known has been working at the telescope.

— Vera C. Rubin (1928–   ), American astronomer

There is a straight ladder from the atom to the grain of sand and the real mystery is the missing rung. Above it, classical physics. Below it, quantum physics. But in between, metaphysics.

— Tom Stoppard (1937–   ), English dramatist,

from his play *Hapgood*, which is replete with ideas from quantum physics

What is man in nature? Nothing in relation to the infinite, all in relation to nothing, a mean between nothing and everything.

What a chimera then is man! What a novelty! What a monster, what a chaos, what a contradiction, what a prodigy! Judge of all things, feeble earthworm, depository of truth, a sink of uncertainty and error, the glory and the shame of the universe.

Man is but a reed, the weakest in nature; but he is a thinking reed.

— Blaise Pascal (1623–1662), French mathematician, physicist and philosopher.

The history of civilization details the steps by which men have succeeded in building up an artificial world within the cosmos. Fragile reed as he may be, man, as Pascal says, is a thinking reed: there lies within him a fund of energy, operating intelligently and so far

akin to that which pervades the universe, that it is competent to influence and modify the cosmic process. In virtue of his intelligence, the dwarf bends the Titan to his will.

– Thomas Henry Huxley (1825–1895), English naturalist

The most incomprehensible thing about the world is that it is comprehensible.

– Albert Einstein (1879–1955)

Nothing troubles me more than time and space; and yet nothing troubles me less, as I never think about them.

– Charles Lamb (1775–1834), English essayist, known, with his sister Mary, for their *Tales from Shakespeare*.

A man said to the universe:
  "Sir, I exist!"
"However," replied the universe,
"That fact has not created in me
A sense of obligation."

– Stephen Crane (1871–1900), American author of Civil War classic, *The Red Badge of Courage*.

I accept the Universe.

– Margaret Fuller (1810–1850), American feminist and critic

By God! she'd better.

– Thomas Carlyle's reputed rejoinder

We know more about the surface of the moon than we do about the bottom of the sea. Having access to that mysterious place will be one of the most exciting things ever to happen. We ought to go [down] 10,000 feet, live there, play there, and travel around. I think it's the only avenue to understanding. I'd like to lure everyone down there to see for themselves. I care about the fate of the plants and animals that share the planet with us. And I care about our own fate. I don't think we'd continue to dump waste in the ocean if we could see what happens to it.

–Sylvia Earle (1935–   ), American marine biologist

5. SCIENCE AND RELIGION

The eye with which I see God is the same eye with which God sees me.

— Meister Eckhart (c.1260–1327), German mystic

I am, as it were, an eye that the cosmos uses to look at itself.

— Rudy Rucker (1946–   ), American mathematician and philosopher. This, and the preceding epigraph, are reminiscent of King Lear's lament: "And take upon us the mystery of things, As if we were God's spies."

Robert W. Fuller

I, Galileo Galilei, aged 70, arraigned before this tribunal of Inquisitors against heretical depravity, swear that I have always believed all that is taught by the Church. But whereas I wrote a book in which I adduce arguments of great cogency ... that the sun is the center of the world and immovable, and that the earth is not the center and moves, I abjure, curse, and detest these errors and heresies and I swear that I will never again assert anything that might furnish occasion for suspicion regarding me.

– Galileo Galilei (1564–1642), Italian astronomer who, threatened with torture by the Inquisition, here recants his belief that the earth moves around the sun (but cannot resist pointing out that his arguments do have "great cogency"). After delivering his retraction, he is said to have whispered under his breath, "But it does move!" He spent the rest of his life under house arrest making further astronomical discoveries and writing books for posterity. In 1992, an ecclesiastical commission appointed by Pope John Paul II acknowledged that Galileo had been right.

I now saw very plainly that these were li eels, or worms, lying all huddled up togeti and wriggling; the whole water seemed to alive with these multifarious animalcules. must say that no more pleasant sight has eve yet come before my eye than these many thou sands of living creatures, seen all alive in a lit tle drop of water, moving among one another, each creature having its own proper motion.

We cannot in any better manner glorify the Lord and Creator of the universe than that in all things, however small they appear to our naked eyes, but which have yet received the gift of life and power of increase, we con template the display of His omnificence and perfections with the utmost admiration.

– Anton van Leeuwenhoek (1632–1723), Dutch scientist, inventor of the microscope, describing the bacteria he was the first to see.

Sire, I found no need for that particular assumption.

– Pierre Simon Laplace (1749–1827), French mathematician and astronomer, in response to

Napoleon, who had asked him what place was left to God in his system of celestial mechanics.

[The 21st] century will be defined by a debate that will run through the remainder of its decades: religion versus science. Religion will lose.

— John McLaughlin (1927–   ), former Jesuit priest and TV talk show host

The writers of the Bible were ... as wise or as ignorant as their generation. Hence it is utterly unimportant that errors of historic or scientific fact should be found in the Bible.

— Monseigneur George Lemaître (1895–1966), Belgian Jesuit priest and physicist, Father of the Big Bang

Science without religion is lame, religion without science is blind.

The Lord God is subtle, but malicious he is not.

I am convinced that [God] does not play dice [with the universe].

My religion consists of a humble admiration of the illimitable superior spirit who reveals himself in the slight details we are able to perceive with our frail and feeble minds.

I am a deeply religious unbeliever.

— Albert Einstein (1879–1955)

The arc of the moral universe is long but it bends toward justice.

— Martin Luther King Jr. (1929–1968), American Civil Rights Leader and Nobel-laureate

Description demands intense observation, so intense that the veil of everyday habit falls away and what we paid no attention to, because it struck us as so ordinary, is revealed as miraculous.

— Czeslaw Milosz (1911–2004), Nobel-laureate Polish poet

Religious feeling is as much a verity as any other part of human consciousness; and

against it, on the subjective side, the waves of science beat in vain.

— John Tyndall (1820–1893), Irish physicist who explained why the sky is blue.

The place where we do our scientific work is a place of prayer.

— Joseph Needham (1900–1995), British biochemist, sinologist, and historian of science

There is a grandeur in this view of life.

— Charles Darwin (1809–1882), English naturalist whose theory of evolution undermined theological dogma more than anything since Copernicus's heliocentric model of the solar system

I asserted that a man has no reason to be ashamed of having an ape for his grandfather. If there were an ancestor whom I should feel shame in recalling it would rather be a man who, not content with an equivocal success in his own sphere of activity, plunges into scientific questions with which he has no real acquaintance, only to obscure them by an aimless rhetoric, and distract the attention of his hearers from the real point at issue by eloquent digressions and skilled appeals to religious prejudice.

– Thomas Henry Huxley (1825–1895), English biologist making an *ad hominem* attack on Bishop Wilberforce for criticizing Darwin's theory of evolution

Basically, everything is one. There is no way in which you can draw a line between things. I think maybe poets have some understanding of this.

Every time I walk on grass I feel sorry, because I know the grass is screaming at me.

– Barbara McClintock (1902–1992), American Nobel prize-winning geneticist

If we do discover a complete theory, it should in time be understandable in broad principle by everyone, not just a few scientists. Then we shall all, philosophers, scientists, and just ordinary people, be able to

take part in the discussion of the question of why it is that we and the universe exist. If we find the answer to that, it would be the ultimate triumph of human reason—for then we would know the mind of God.

– Stephen Hawking (1930–   ), British physicist and author a best-selling but seldom-read book *A Brief History of Time*. The film version is more accessible.

You can talk about people like Buddha, Jesus, Moses, and Confucius, but the thing that really convinced me that such people exist were conversations with Niels Bohr.

– John A. Wheeler (1911–1908), leading American physicist who co-authored a seminal paper on nuclear fission with Niels Bohr

Medicine makes people ill, mathematics makes them sad, and theology makes them sinful.

– Martin Luther (1483–1546), German Protestant reformer

Formerly, when religion was strong and science weak, men mistook magic for medicine; now, when science is strong and religion weak, men mistake medicine for magic.

If you talk to God, you are praying; if God talks to you, you have schizophrenia.

– Thomas Szasz (1920–   ), Hungarian-born American psychiatrist and writer

It is a strange and long war, the war that violence is forever waging against truth. All the efforts of violence are powerless to weaken truth, and serve only to make it stronger. All the lights of truth are powerless to stop violence, and serve only to make it angrier. Do not suppose, however, that the two are equal: there is one very great difference between them. The course of violence is directed by God who channels its effects to the exaltation of the truth it attacks; where truth subsists eternally and in the end triumphs over all its enemies, for it is eternal and powerful as God himself.

– Blaise Pascal (1623–1662), French scientist and philosopher

Robert W. Fuller

Though much has been written foolishly about the antagonism of science and religion, there is indeed no such antagonism. What all these world religions declare by inspiration and insight, history as it grows clear and science as its range extends display, as a reasonable and demonstrable fact, that men form one universal brotherhood, that they spring from one common origin, that their individual lives, their nations and races, interbreed and blend and go on to merge again at last in one common human destiny upon this little planet amidst the stars.

– H. G. Wells (1866–1946), British writer, from his *Outline of History* written in 1920.

Awe is an intuition of the dignity of all things, a realization that things not only are what they are but also stand, however remotely, for something supreme.

– Abraham Heschel (1907–1972), Polish-born American rabbi and philosopher

6. SCIENCE AND POLITICS

Nationalism is an infantile sickness. It is the measles of the human race.

I am an absolute pacifist. It is a feeling that possesses me, because murder is disgusting.

If my theory of relativity is proven correct, Germany will claim me as a German and France will declare that I am a citizen of the world. Should my theory prove untrue, France will say that I am a German and Germany will declare that I am a Jew.

    – Albert Einstein (1879–1955)

After all, science is essentially international, and it is only through lack of the historical sense that national qualities have been attributed to it.

— Marie Curie (1867–1934), Polish-born French physicist who twice won the Nobel prize, for isolating radioactive elements

There is no national science just as there is no national multiplication table; what is national is no longer science.

— Anton Chekhov (1860–1904), Russian physician and dramatist

The exiled mathematician — and who among us can today feel free from the danger of exile — can find everywhere the modest livelihood which allows him to pursue his work. Even in jail one can do good mathematics if one's courage fail him not.

— André Weil (1906–1998), French mathematician who did fundamental work while in prison for refusing service in the French army

Social thinking has no more important task before it than that of taking adequate account of cultural relativism. The recognition of cultural relativism carries with it its own values, which need not be those of absolutist philosophies. It challenges customary opinions and causes those who have been bred to them acute discomfort. [It accepts] as grounds of hope and as a new basis for tolerance the coexisting and equally valid patterns of life which mankind has created for itself from the raw materials of existence.

– Ruth Benedict (1887–1948), American anthropologist. This quote is from the final passage in her influential book *Patterns of Culture*, published in 1934, which taught that cultures are integrated wholes—each culture a "personality writ large"—and accordingly that one's native culture should not unconsciously be taken as an absolute standard to which others ought necessarily aspire. Published as Hitler came to power, her ideas remain a powerful antidote to chauvinism, nationalism, and racism.

When our fellow citizens—even while they are very young—are hung up on the idea of a career at any price, then this is an alarm signal. The sirens are screaming! Because the readiness to pay any price signifies a profound indiscriminateness and indifference to other people — towards everyone except oneself.

A thermonuclear war cannot be considered a continuation of politics by other means. It would be a means to universal suicide.

– Andrei D. Sakharov (1921–1989), Nobel-laureate Russian physicist (father of Soviet H-bomb), and human rights activist. Sakharov belongs with Gandhi, Martin Luther King Jr., and Nelson Mandela as one of the moral giants of the twentieth century.

The social addiction to armaments races is not fundamentally different from individual addiction to drugs. Common sense urges the addict always to get another fix. And so on.

– Gregory Bateson (1904–1980), English-born American anthropologist

Either man is obsolete, or war is.

– Buckminster Fuller (1895–1983), American engineer who illuminated our predicament with his resonant phrase "Spaceship Earth"

Error-tolerance is the hallmark of natural ecological communities, of free market economies, and of open societies. I believe it must have been a primary quality of life from the very beginning.

– Freeman Dyson, British-born American physicist and writer

*To make vicious and abandoned people happy, it has generally been supposed necessary, **first**, to make them virtuous. But why not reverse this order! Why not make them first **happy**, and then virtuous!*

– Count Rumford (1753–1814), Anglo-American scientist whose many practical inventions revolutionized household life, e. g., central heating, the smokeless chimney, the kitchen oven, the pressure cooker, the drip coffeepot. He was also a social innovator, bringing his scientific ingenuity to bear on urban problems of poverty and public education.

7. THE USES OF SCIENCE

Nature, and Nature's laws lay hid in night:
God said, 'Let Newton be!' and all was light.

– Alexander Pope (1688–1744), British poet

It did not last: the Devil howling 'Ho!
Let Einstein be!' restored the status quo.

– John Collings Squire (1884–1958), British journalist

The dreams of reason bring forth monsters.

– Francisco José de Goya (1746–1828), Spanish painter

Whenever science makes a discovery, the devil grabs it while the angels are debating the best way to use it.

— Alan Valentine (1901–1980), American author and university president

Technology is a queer thing. It brings you great gifts with one hand, and it stabs you in the back with the other.

— C. P. Snow (1905–1980), English physicist, scientific statesman, and novelist

The content of physics is the concern of physicists, its effect the concern of all men.

— Frederick Dürrenmatt (1921–1990), Swiss writer

To the politician, the scientist is like a trained monkey who goes up the coconut tree to bring down choice coconuts. If he is successful in bringing down a very choice one, the owner of the monkey begins to worry, lest somebody else learn the trick. The

priest is in the same position. He is asked to bless the arms of the nation; he is not asked what the nation should do with those arms. [Scientists and religious leaders] are exactly in the same place.

. – I. I. Rabi (1898–1988), American Nobel-laureate physicist and scientific statesman. Witnessed first test of atomic bomb and advised the U. S. government on science policy.

The unleashed power of the atom has changed everything save our modes of thinking and we thus drift toward unparalleled catastrophe.

– Albert Einstein

In some sort of crude sense which no vulgarity, no humor, no overstatement can quite extinguish, the physicists have known sin; and this is a knowledge which they cannot lose.

– J. Robert Oppenheimer (1904–1967), American nuclear physicist, "Father of the atom bomb." (The reaction of many physicists to this controversial remark was, "Speak for yourself, 'Oppie'.")

People must understand that science is inherently neither a potential for good nor for evil. It is a potential to be harnessed by man to do his bidding.

– Glenn Seaborg (1912–1999), American nuclear chemist and scientific statesman, discoverer of plutonium and other transuranic elements.

Birth is the most hazardous time of life.

– Virginia Apgar (1909–1974), developer of the "Apgar score," a test of vital signs given worldwide to newborns during the first minute of life to see if emergency measures are indicated.

I was bothered by the fact that thalidomide would not put a horse to sleep.

– Frances Kelsey (1914–   ), American research physician whose suspicions kept thalidomide—Europe's favorite sleeping pill—from the United States market and thus prevented thousands of birth defects.

At temperatures above freezing one is between the Scylla of excessive drying and the Charybdis of molds.

– Mary Pennington (1872–1952), American bacteriologist whose research on refrigeration led to a revolution in the preservation of perishable foods.

Before a war military science seems a real science, like astronomy. But after a war it seems more like astrology.

– Rebecca West (1892–1983), Irish writer

Though many have tried, no one has ever yet explained away the decisive fact that science, which can do so much, cannot decide what it ought to do.

– Joseph Wood Krutch (1893–1970), American critic

Science increases our power in proportion as it lowers our pride.

– Claude Bernard (1813–1878), French physiologist

Science must constantly be reminded that her purposes are not the only purposes and that the order of uniform causation which she has use for, and is therefore right in postulating, may be enveloped in a wider order, on which she has no claim at all.

— William James (1842–1910), American philosopher and psychologist. He posed the question, "Is there a moral equivalent of war?"

The Three Laws of Robotics:

1. A robot may not injure a human being, or, through inaction, allow a human being to come to harm.

2. A robot must obey orders given it by human beings, except where such orders would conflict with the First Law.

3. A robot must protect its own existence as long as such protection does not conflict with the First or Second Law.

— Isaac Asimov (1920–1992), Russian-born American writer and futurist who coined the term "robotics."

The future offers very little hope for those who expect that our new mechanical slaves will offer us a world in which we may rest from thinking. Help us they may, but at the cost of supreme demands upon our honesty and our intelligence. The world of the future will be an ever more demanding struggle against the limitations of our intelligence, not a comfortable hammock in which we can lie down to be waited upon by our robot slaves.

We can be humble and live a good life with the aid of machines, or we can be arrogant and die.

– Norbert Wiener (1894–1964), American mathematician

8. SCIENCE AND THE ARTS

To see a world in a grain of sand
And a heaven in a wild flower,
Hold infinity in the palm of your hand
And eternity in an hour.

– William Blake (1757–1827), English poet, painter and mystic

A modern poet has characterized the perso-nality of art and the impersonality of science as follows: Art is I; Science is We.

– Claude Bernard (1813-1878), French physiologist

Art upsets, science reassures.

– Georges Braque (1882–1963), French Cubist painter

There exists a passion for comprehension just as there exists a passion for music. That passion is rather common in children, but gets lost in most people later on. Without this passion there would be neither mathematics nor natural science.

The most beautiful experience we can have is the mysterious ... the fundamental emotion which stands at the cradle of true art and true science.

– Albert Einstein

Computers are useless. They can only give you answers.

– Pablo Picasso (1881–1973), Spanish painter. Like many artists, he preferred questions to answers.

Euclid alone has looked on Beauty bare.

    – Edna St. Vincent Millay (1892–1950), American poet and feminist

Beauty is the first test: there is no permanent place in the world for ugly mathematics.

    – G. H. Hardy (1877–1947), English mathematician

Mathematics, rightly viewed, possesses not only truth, but supreme beauty, a beauty cold and austere, like that of sculpture, without appeal to any part of our weaker nature, without the gorgeous trappings of painting or music, yet sublimely pure, and capable of a stern perfection such as only the greatest art can show.

    – Bertrand Russell (1872–1970), Welsh mathematician, philosopher and, in his later years, political activist

I believe the intellectual life of the whole of western society is increasingly being split into two polar groups. Literary intellectuals at one

pole—at the other scientists, and as the most representative, the physical scientists. Between the two a gulf of mutual incomprehension.

A good many times I have been present at gatherings of people who, by the standards of the traditional culture, are thought highly educated and who have with considerable gusto been expressing their incredulity at the illiteracy of scientists. Once or twice I have been provoked and have asked the company how many of them could describe the Second Law of Thermodynamics. The response was cold: it was also negative.

– C. P. Snow (1905–1980), author of *The Two Cultures* and *The Scientific Revolution*

The true men of action in our time, those who transform the world, are not the politicians and statesmen, but the scientists. When I find myself in the company of scientists, I feel like a shabby curate who has strayed by mistake into a drawing room full of dukes.

– W. H. Auden (1907–1973), English poet

There was a young lady named Bright,
Whose speed was far faster than light;
She set out one day
In a relative way,
And returned the previous night.

     – Arthur H. R. Buller (1874–1944), British botanist

Big whirls have little whirls,
That feed on their velocity;
And little whirls have lesser whirls,
And so on to viscosity.

     – Lewis F. Richardson (1881– 1953), English mathematician and meteorologist who pioneered weather forecasting

He who would do good to another must do it
in minute particulars;
General good is the plea of the scoundrel,
hypocrite, and flatterer:
For art and science cannot exist but in mi-
nutely organized particulars.

Time and Space are Real Beings, a Male and a Female. Time is a Man; Space is a Woman.

– William Blake (1757–1827), English painter and poet

.

9. MATHEMATICS QUEEN OF THE SCIENCES

Mathematics is the queen of the sciences.

– Carl Frederick Gauss (1777–1855), German mathematician, astronomer, and physicist

God ever geometrizes.

– Plato (c.428–c.348 BCE), Greek philosopher.

Let no one ignorant of mathematics enter this door.

– Sign above entrance to Plato's Academy, a famous center for philosophical, mathematical, and scientific work.

There is nothing in the world except empty, curved space. Matter, charge, electromagnetism, and other fields are only manifestations of the bending of space. Physics is geometry.

– John Archibald Wheeler (1911–1908), American pioneer in nuclear and gravitation physics, who did much to prove Plato's claim—that God is a geometer—prescient.

Philosophy is written in this grand book—I mean the universe—which stands continually open to our gaze, but it cannot be understood unless one first learns to comprehend the language in which it is written. It is written in the language of mathematics.

– Galileo Galilei (1564–1642), Italian astronomer

When you can measure what you are speaking about and express it in numbers, you know something about it; but when you cannot measure it, when you cannot express it in numbers, your knowledge is of a meager, unsatisfactory kind.

There is nothing new to be discovered in physics now. All that remains is more and more precise measurement.

– Lord Kelvin (1824–1907), Irish-born Scottish physicist after whom the absolute ("Kelvin") temperature scale is named.

There is no branch of mathematics, however abstract, that may not someday be applied to phenomena of the real world.

– Nikolai Lobachevski (1792–1856), Russian discoverer of non-Euclidean geometry

Numerical precision is the very soul of science.

The perfection of mathematical beauty is such that whatsoever is most beautiful and regular is also found to be most useful and excellent.

– Sir D'Arcy Thompson (1860–1948), Scottish mathematical biologist

All the pictures which science now draws of nature and which alone seem capable of according with observational fact are mathemat-

ical pictures. From the intrinsic evidence of his creation, the Great Architect of the Universe now begins to appear as a pure mathematician, and the universe begins to look more like a great thought than a great machine.

– Sir James Jeans (1877–1946), English physicist, astronomer, and writer

It seems to be one of the fundamental features of nature that fundamental physical laws are described in terms of a mathematical theory of great beauty and power, needing quite a high standard of mathematics for one to understand it. You may wonder: Why is nature constructed along these lines? One could perhaps describe the situation by saying that God is a mathematician of a very high order, and He used very advanced mathematics in constructing the universe. Our feeble attempts at mathematics enable us to understand a bit of the universe, and as we proceed to develop higher and higher mathematics we can hope to understand the universe better.

– Paul A. M. Dirac (1902–1984), English

Nobel prize-winning mathematical physicist, pioneer of quantum theory

Because the shape of the whole universe is most perfect and, in fact, designed by the wisest creator, nothing in all of the world will occur in which no maximum or minimum rule is somehow shining forth.

    – Leonhard Euler (1707–1783), Swiss mathematician who developed the mathematics of extremes

God made the whole numbers—all the rest is the work of man.

    – Leopold Kronecker (1823–1891), German mathematician

As far as the mathematical theorems refer to reality, they are not sure, and as far as they are sure, they do not refer to reality.

    – Albert Einstein (1879–1955)

10. SCIENTISTS – ON THEMSELVES AND THEIR COLLEAGUES

When shall I cease from wondering?

  – Galileo Galilei (1564–1642), Italian discoverer of Jupiter's moons, sunspots, and much more

*I thank thee, O Lord, our Creator, that thou
hast permitted me to look at the beauty in
thy work of creation; I exult in the works of
thy hands. See, I have completed the work to
which I felt called; I have earned interest
from the talent that thou hast given me. I
have proclaimed the glory of thy works to*

the people who will read these demonstra-
tions, to the extent that the limitations of my
spirit would allow.

— Johann Kepler (1571–1630), German discoverer of the laws of planetary motion

As soon as I was old enough to throw off the
yoke of my teachers, I dropped the study of
letters, and, resolving to pursue no know-
ledge anywhere but within myself or in the
great book of life, I spent the rest of my
youth traveling.

— René Descartes (1596–1650), French mathematician, whose pronouncement "Cogito
ergo sum" [I think, therefore I am] is claimed by
some to have opened the way to scientific
progress, and by others simply to have
spawned more derivative quotations than any
other saying in history, with the possible excep-
tion of T. S. Eliot's epitaph for humankind: "Not
with a bang but a whimper."

The man who opens for the first time a
doorway into the future and who hears faint
and far off, like surf on unknown reefs, the

tumult and magnificence of an age beyond his own is confronted not alone with the scorn of his less perceptive fellows, but even with the problem of finding the words to impose his vision upon contemporaries inclined to the belief that the world's time is short and its substance far sunk into decay.

– Loren Eisely (1907–1977), science writer describing Sir Francis Bacon, the first great statesman of science. The description fits many scientific forerunners.

Newton regarded the universe as a cryptogram set by the Almighty. By pure thought, the riddle, he believed, would be revealed to the initiate.

– John Maynard Keynes (1883–1946), English economist

I do not know what I may appear to the world, but to myself I seem to have been only like a boy playing on the seashore, and diverting myself in now and then finding a smoother pebble or a prettier shell than or-

dinary, whilst the great ocean of truth lay all undiscovered before me.

If I have seen farther it is by standing on the shoulders of giants.

— Isaac Newton (1642–1727), great English physicist. When not speaking for posterity he was often not so humble.

I transmit but I do not create; I am sincerely fond of the ancient.

— Confucius (551–479 BCE), as transmitted by John A. Wheeler

Every other Jewish mother in Brooklyn would ask her child after school: "So? Did you learn anything today?" But not my mother. "Izzy," she would say, "did you ask a good question today?"

— Isidore I. Rabi (1898–1988), American Nobel-laureate physicist and scientific states-man, famous for his puckish humor. At 77 he gave his age as "three score plus ten plus ten percent."

A good scientist is a person in whom the child-hood quality of perennial curiosity lingers on. Once he gets an answer, he has other questions.

– Frederick Seitz (1911–2008), American physicist, who could well have been describing I. I. Rabi

The best scientist is open to experience and begins with romance—the idea that anything is possible. Touch a scientist and you touch a child.

– Ray Bradbury (1920–2012), American science-fiction writer

I am actually not at all a man of science, not an observer, not an experimenter, not a thinker. I am by temperament nothing but a conquistador—an adventurer.

– Sigmund Freud (1856–1939), Austrian neurologist and founder of psychoanalysis

To create a true sketch of my life is impossible, since leaving out relations with women

in my case creates on the one hand a great void, and on the other hand seems to be required, firstly on account of scandal, secondly because they are hardly of sufficient interest, thirdly because in such matters no man is really completely sincere and truthful, nor ought he to be.

— Erwin Schrödinger (1887–1961), Austrian physicist, creator of wave mechanics and a lover of women. Though acknowledgment of the role of lovers in the creative arts is not uncommon, Schrödinger's avowal of the importance of his relationships with women to his creative process is rare among scientists. Walter Moore, in his biography *Schrödinger: Life and Thought*, breaks new ground by writing about his subject's scientific life *and* his love life. Both were prodigious.

One is never again as intelligent as one is at sixteen.

— Leo Szilard (1898–1964), Hungarian-born American nuclear physicist. Szilard drafted the historic letter which Einstein sent to President Roosevelt alerting him to the possibility of building an atomic bomb.

There are two kinds of Nobel prize winners: the kind that make the prize famous, and the kind that are made famous by the prize. I am of the latter variety.

– Polykarp Kusch (1911–1993), American Nobel-laureate physicist, remembered with amusement by dozing students at whom he threw chalk.

I learned much from my teachers, more from my colleagues, and most of all from my students.

– Eugene P. Wigner (1902–1995), Hungarian-born American Nobel-laureate nuclear physicist, quoting from the Talmud

But it isn't even wrong.

Wolfgang Pauli (1900–58), Austrian-born American Nobel-laureate physicist. Pauli, famous for his acerbity, is said to have made this comment at the conclusion of a seminar he found boring. I once saw him reduce a post-doctoral fellow, who'd just presented his latest work, to tears. Robert Oppenheimer, taking pity, interceded and shut Pauli up, to the immense relief of the audience.

I've just been reading some of my early papers, and you know, when I'd finished I said to myself, "Rutherford, my boy, you used to be a damned clever fellow."

– Ernest Rutherford (1871–1937), British pioneer nuclear physicist

Let us have "sweet girl graduates" by all means. They will be none the less sweet for a little wisdom; and the "golden hair" will not curl less gracefully outside the head by reason of there being brains within.

– Thomas Henry Huxley (1825–1895), English biologist poking fun at those who opposed admitting women to University.

To the professor, whose name I do not know, who was the only one to vote for my admission to the school, thus protesting the prejudice which would exclude women from advanced studies.

– Mary Corinna Putnam Jacobi, first woman graduate of the École de Médecine in Paris. This is the dedication to her doctoral dissertation presented in 1871.

It is to be regretted that she had been induced to depart from the appropriate sphere of her sex and led to aspire to honors and duties which, by the order of nature and the common consent of the world, devolves alone upon men.

– *Boston Medical and Surgical Journal*, commenting upon the award of an M. D. degree to Elizabeth Blackwell, the first woman doctor in the United States.

The world cannot afford the loss of the talents of half of its people if we are to solve the many problems which beset us.

Whatever women do, they must do twice as well as men to be thought half as good. Luckily, this is not difficult.

– Rosalyn Yalow (1921–2011), Nobel-laureate medical researcher

It would be expected that the discovery of imaginary numbers, which seem nearer to madness than to logic and which, in fact, has

illuminated all mathematical science, would come from such a man whose adventurous life was not always commendable from the moral point of view, and who from childhood suffered from fantastic hallucinations ... .

– Jacques Hadamard (1865–1963), French mathematician, speaking of Jerome Cardan, who introduced imaginary numbers into mathematics in the seventeenth century.

The longing to behold harmony is the source of the inexhaustible patience and perseverance with which Planck has devoted himself to the most general problems of our science. The state of mind which enables a man to do work of this kind is akin to that of the religious worshipper or the lover; the daily effort comes from no deliberate intention or program, but straight from the heart.

– Albert Einstein speaking of Max Planck (1858–1947), German Nobel-laureate physicist, father of modern quantum theory

As an older friend I must advise you against it for in the first place you will not succeed; and even if you succeed, no one will believe you.

– Max Planck to Einstein upon learning of his intention to develop a general theory of relativity.

*Anybody who has been seriously engaged in scientific work of any kind realizes that over the entrance to the gates of the temple of science are written the words: **Ye must have faith**. It is a quality which the scientist cannot dispense with.*

– Max Planck

When I choose post-doctoral students to work with me now, I tend to choose the ones who are most energetic. They all know enough and most are bright enough. But to make brilliant discoveries, you have to be hardworking. If you're awfully bright, it may help. But mostly you have to be willing to do the work and to persevere through periods of doubt.

– Vera C. Rubin, American astronomer

Newton himself was better aware of the weaknesses inherent in this intellectual edifice than the generations which followed him. This fact has always roused my admiration.

Only the genius of Riemann, solitary and uncomprehended, had already won its way by the middle of the last century to a new conception of space, in which space was deprived of its rigidity, and in which its power to take part in physical events was recognized as possible. (Bernhard Riemann (1826–1866), German mathematician, created the non-Euclidean geometry Einstein used to formulate his general theory of relativity.)

[Bohr] utters his opinions like one perpetually groping and never like one who believes he is in possession of definite truth.

I sometimes ask myself how it came about that I was the one to develop the theory of relativity. The reason, I think, is that a normal adult never stops to think about problems of space and time. These are things which he has thought of as a child. But my intellectual development was retarded, as a result of which I began to wonder about space and time only when I had already grown up.

I live in that solitude which is painful in youth, but delicious in the years of maturity.

*I want to go when **I** want. It is tasteless to prolong life artificially. I have done my share, it is time to go. I will do it elegantly.*

– Albert Einstein (1879–1955). The last of these Einstein quotes was spoken to his housekeeper after Einstein had suffered a stroke. He refused all suggestions for an operation and died within a few days.

11. QUESTIONS, GUESSES, AND PRE-DICTIONS

First you guess. Don't laugh, this is the most important step. Then you compute the consequences. Compare the consequences to experience. If it disagrees with experience, the guess is wrong. In that simple statement is the key to science. It doesn't matter how beautiful your guess is or how smart you are or what your name is. If it disagrees with experience, it's wrong. That's all there is to it.

— Richard Feynman (1918–1988), Nobel-laureate American physicist

As to science itself, it can only grow.

    – Galileo Galilei, writing in 1632

What would the world look like if I rode on a beam of light?

Is the universe friendly?

    – Albert Einstein (1879–1955), who created the theory of relativity to answer his first question.

What is Life?

    – Title of a path-breaking book, published in 1944 by Nobel-laureate physicist Erwin Schrödinger, which helped spawn the field of molecular biology.

In the future, as in the past, the great ideas must be simplifying ideas.

    – André Weil, French mathematician

The catastrophe of the atomic bombs which shook men out of cities and businesses and economic relations, shook them also out of their old-established habits of thought, and out of the lightly held beliefs and prejudices that came down to them from the past.

– H. G. Wells (1866–1946), British futurist, writing in *1914*!

Every sentence I utter should be regarded by you not as an assertion, but as a question.

– Niels Bohr (1885–1962), who began lectures with this warning.

I believe that in about fifty years it will be possible to program computers to [imitate human beings] so well that an average interrogator will not have more than 70% chance of making the right identification [i.e., distinguishing between a human and a computer interlocutor] after five minutes of questioning. I believe that at the end of the century one will be able to speak of machines thinking without expecting to be contradicted.

– Alan Turing (1912–1954), English mathematician and computer pioneer, speaking to journalists in 1950.

How is it that I am a collection of a hundred billion nerve cells, yet I think and act as one?

— Rodolfo Llinás (1934–   ), Colombian neuroscientist

Will we, who have the knowledge of many ways, leave our children free to choose among them?

— Margaret Mead (1901–1978), American anthropologist. From the closing lines of her 1928 classic *Coming of Age in Samoa.*

We shall, sooner or later, arrive at a mechanical equivalent of consciousness.

— Thomas Henry Huxley (1825–1895), English biologist

Some recent work ... leads me to expect that the element uranium may be turned into a new and important source of energy in the immediate future. Certain aspects of the situation ... seem to call for watchfulness and, if necessary, quick action on the part of the

Administration. ... [I]t may become possible to set up a nuclear chain reaction in a large mass of uranium, by which vast amounts of power ... would be generated. ... This new phenomenon would also lead to the construction of ... extremely powerful bombs of a new type....

– Albert Einstein, from a letter sent to President Roosevelt in August 1939, drafted for him by Hungarian-born physicist Leo Szilard. It led to the Manhattan project, the World War II effort to construct an atomic bomb.

On July 16, 1945, I was out in the desert in New Mexico ... awaiting the tests of the first large-scale release of atomic energy. The site chosen had been named "Journey of Death" hundreds of years ago. Nine miles away, there was a tower about one hundred feet high. On top of that tower was a little shack. In that shack was a bomb. This particular morning it was set to go off. The announcer said, "Thirty seconds"—"ten seconds"— and we were lying there, very tense, in the early dawn, and there were just a few streaks of gold in the east. Those were the longest ten seconds I ever experienced. Suddenly, there was an enormous flash of light, the brightest light I have ever seen. It blasted; it pounced; it bored its way into you. It was a vision which was seen with more than the eye. It was seen to last forever. You would wish it would stop. Finally it was over, and we looked toward the place where the bomb had been; there was an enormous ball of fire which grew and grew and it rolled as it grew; it went up into the air, in yellow flashes and into scarlet and green. It looked menacing. It seemed to come towards one.

A new thing had just been born; a new control; a new understanding which man had acquired over nature. That was the scientific opening of the atomic age.

The most serious thing about the atomic bomb, even today, is its amazing cheapness. I costs less than one-tenth as much money to destroy a square mile by atomic bombing as it does by ordinary bombing. Even the poor nation can afford to be destructive.

– I. I. Rabi (1898–1988), American Nobel-laureate physicist and scientific statesman. He won the betting pool, held by scientists witnessing the first atomic test, for the most accurate prediction of the energy released by the bomb. His implied prediction regarding nuclear proliferation looks equally prescient.

People will build a rocket ship which can fly so fast and go up so high, that it then stays up all by itself and circles the Earth like a moon. From such a flying apparatus one can then oversee all parts of the Earth as on a map.

– A note made in 1946 by Kurt Gödel (1906–1978) on a conversation with Albert Einstein during one of their daily walks in Princeton. Many mathematicians view Gödel's results in mathematical logic much as physicists do Einstein's in physics—as unsurpassed in their fundamental importance. Newton had foreseen artificial satellites as a theoretical possibility about three centuries earlier. With the wartime development of rockets, satellites would soon be a reality. The childlike awe, in what is a conversation—between two of the most original scientific minds of all time—is itself noteworthy.

I ask you to look both ways. For the road to a knowledge of the stars leads through the atom; and important knowledge of the atom has been reached through the stars.

– Arthur Stanley Eddington (1882-1944), English astronomer whose measurements provided early confirmation of Einstein's general theory of relativity. This is a prediction not *of* physics, but rather about the *development* of physics. As theories of the cosmos and the atom converge, it looks ever more prophetic.

The more important fundamental laws and facts of physical science have all been discovered, and these are now so firmly established that the possibility of their ever being supplanted ...is exceedingly remote.

– A. A. Michelson (1852–1931), American physicist, writing in 1903. Surprisingly, there have been few generations in which such predictions haven't been made. Someone is always (erroneously) proclaiming the end of something: physics, science, history! The irony in this case is that it was precisely Michelson's experiments on light which set Einstein on the road to relativity.

If an elderly but distinguished scientist says that something is possible he is almost certainly right, but if he says that it is impossible he is very probably wrong.

– Arthur C. Clarke (1917–2008), English futurist, who originated the idea of communications satellites and authored *2001: A Space Odyssey*

As long as there are sovereign nations possessing great power, war is inevitable.

All of these [research] endeavors are based on the belief that existence should have a completely harmonious structure. Today we have less ground than ever before for allowing ourselves to be forced away from this wonderful belief.

– Albert Einstein, pessimistic and optimistic

It is a curious situation that the sea, from which life first arose, should now be threatened by the activities of one form of that life. But the sea, though changed in a sinister

way, will continue to exist; the threat is ra-
ther to life itself.

– Rachel Carson (1907–1964), American marine biologist and writer. Her writings, among them *The Sea Around Us* in 1951 and *Silent Spring* in 1962, played seminal roles in creating the environmental movement.

A butterfly's capricious flight may result in a tropical storm, not tomorrow, but one or two years down the road. This is why long-range weather forecasting is so difficult: everything, absolutely everything, must be taken into account. No perturbation can be deemed too small to have any influence.

– Ivar Ekeland (1944–   ), mathematician, explaining the difficulty of predicting certain behaviors of complex (chaotic) systems.

All history is the history of physics.

– Oswald Spengler (1880–1936), German author of *Decline of the West.* In this provocative assertion, Spengler is pointing out the link between technological innovation and political power. For example, pre-historic metallurgical discoveries ushered in the iron and bronze ages; the modern era has been dubbed the "atomic age" and the "age of information."

The machines will get good enough at dealing with complexity that they can start dealing with their own complexity, and you'll get systems that evolve.

We're building a machine that will be proud of us.

    – Daniel Hillis (1956–   ), American computer scientist and co-founder of Thinking Machines Corporation

[Someday human intelligence] might be viewed as a historically interesting, albeit peripheral, special case of machine intelligence.

    – Pierre Baldi (1967–   ), computer scientist

We hope to explain the entire universe in a single, simple formula that you can wear on your T-shirt.

    – Leon Lederman, American Nobel-laureate physicist

12. SIMPLE TRUTHS

Above all, do no harm.

A wise man should ... learn how by his own thought to derive benefit from his illnesses.

– Hippocrates (c. 460–400 BCE), Greek physician

Nothing is permanent but change.

Character is destiny.

– Heraclitus of Ephesus (c. 500 BCE), Greek philosopher who taught, "You can never step into the same river twice."

The trouble is that the balls go where you throw them.

– Jugglers' saying

GIGO.

– Computer programmers' motto ("Garbage In, Garbage Out").

The simple is the seal of the true.

– Inscription in physics auditorium of the University of Göttingen.

Beauty is the splendor of truth.

– Latin motto, applied instinctively by scientists seeking new truths.

Fortune favors the prepared mind.

– Louis Pasteur (1822–1895), French chemist and discoverer of vaccinations against smallpox and other diseases. (Cf. "Luck is the residue of design." – Branch Rickey, baseball magnate.)

Dare to be naive.

– Buckminster Fuller (1895–1983), American engineer who built geodesic domes and coined the phrase "Spaceship Earth"

Maybe that's why young people make success. They don't know enough. Because when you know enough it's obvious that every idea that you have is not good.

We are not that much smarter than each other.

– Richard P. Feynman (1918–1988), American Nobel-laureate physicist, who demonstrated on national television that frozen O-rings had led to the explosion of space shuttle Challenger

A clash of doctrines is not a disaster, it is an opportunity.

– Alfred North Whitehead (1861–1947), English mathematician and philosopher and co-author with Bertrand Russell of the classic of logic, *Principia Mathematica*. Imagine a world wherein we viewed political disagreements in this way. It would be a world in which inquiry was regarded as a better game than war.

When you are courting a nice girl an hour seems like a second. When you sit on a red-hot cinder a second seems like an hour. That's relativity.

– Albert Einstein

Time is God's way of keeping things from happening all at once.

– graffiti

The only medicine for suffering, crime, and all the other woes of mankind, is wisdom.

– Thomas Henry Huxley (1825–1895), English biologist

What everyone believed yesterday, and you believe today, only cranks will believe tomorrow.

– Francis Crick (1916–2004), co-discoverer of the molecular structure of the gene. This remark was directed at believers in "vitalism"— the doctrine that there exists some specific life force which cannot be understood in terms of physics and chemistry—but it has much more general applicability.

Without a theory the facts are silent.

— Friedrich Hayek (1899–1992), Austrian economist and philosopher

The map is not the territory.

— Alfred Korzybski (1879–1950), Polish-born American philosopher's pithy reminder that representations (e.g., models and theories) should never be confused with reality.

To have a name is to be.

— Benoit Mandelbrot (1924–2010), Polish-born American mathematician known for fractals

Human history becomes more and more a race between education and catastrophe.

— H. G. Wells (1866–1946), British writer, from his *Outline of History* written in 1920

I have discovered that all human misery comes only from this, that we are incapable of staying quietly in a room.

There are two equally dangerous extremes—
to shut reason out, and to let nothing else in.

The heart has its reasons which reason does
not know.

– Blaise Pascal (1623–62), French mathematician, physicist, philosopher

ABOUT THE AUTHOR

Robert W. Fuller earned his Ph.D. in physics at Princeton University and taught at Columbia, where he co-authored *Mathematics of Classical and Quantum Physics*. He then served as president of Oberlin College, his alma mater. For a dozen years, beginning in 1978, he worked in what came to be known as "citizen diplomacy" to improve the Cold War relationship. During the 1990s, he served as board chair of the global NGO Internews, which promotes democracy via free and independent media. In 2004 he was elected a Fellow of the World Academy of Art and Science, and in 2011 he served as keynote speaker at the National Conference on Dignity for All hosted by the president of Bangladesh. With the end of the Cold War and the collapse of the USSR, Fuller looked back on his career and understood that he had been, at different times in his life, a somebody and a nobody. His periodic sojourns into "Nobodyland" led him to identify and probe rankism—abuse of the power inherent in rank—and ultimately to write *Somebodies and Nobodies: Overcoming the Abuse of Rank* (New Society Publishers, 2003). Three years later, he published a sequel focusing on building a "dignitarian" society, titled *All Rise: Somebodies, Nobodies, and the Politics of Dignity* (Berrett-Koehler, 2006). An Indian edition was published in 2007 (Viveka Foundation), a Chinese translation in 2008, and a Bengali translation in 2009. With co-author Pamela Gerloff, Fuller has also published *Dignity for All: How to Create a World Without Rankism*. His most recent books are *Religion and Science: A Beautiful Friendship?; Genomes, Menomes, Wenomes: Neuroscience and Human Dignity; The Rowan Tree: A Novel;* and *Belonging: A Memoir.*

Connect with Robert W. Fuller Online

Web site: www.robertworksfuller.com
Facebook: www.facebook.com/robertwfuller
Twitter: twitter.com/#!/robertwfuller

Other Books by Robert W. Fuller

Mathematics of Classical and Quantum Physics
(with Frederick W. Byron, Jr.)

Somebodies and Nobodies:
Overcoming the Abuse of Rank

All Rise:
Somebodies, Nobodies, and the Politics of Dignity

Dignity for All:
How to Create a World Without Rankism
(with Pamela A. Gerloff)

Religion and Science: A Beautiful Friendship?

Genomes, Menomes, Wenomes:
Neuroscience and Human Dignity

The Rowan Tree: A Novel

Belonging: A Memoir

For readers who want to explore dignity as a foundation for interpersonal and international relations, Robert W. Fuller's novel *The Rowan Tree* is now available as an ebook, a paperback, and an audiobook at: www.rowantreenovel.com

As Arthurian myth sowed seeds of democracy, *The Rowan Tree* foretells an international culture of dignity. Anchored by two interlocking love stories, this unflinching novel of ideas brims with passionate quests, revelatory failures, and inextinguishable hope.

The Rowan Tree is an inspirational tour de force that reaches from the rebellious American '60s into humanity's global future. Soul-searching treks around the world intersect with campus revolution, basketball, math, ballet, and a destined rise to the White House. Love runs ahead of politics and lights the way for nations to follow.